Then *&* Now
Whitstable

Then & Now
Whitstable

Mick Glover

Frontispiece: The 'Human Analyst' amusement machine outside Tower Amusements, *c.* 1930.

First published in 2005 by Tempus Publishing

Reprinted in 2010 by
The History Press
The Mill, Brimscombe Port,
Stroud, Gloucestershire, GL5 2QG
www.thehistorypress.co.uk

British Library Cataloguing in Publication Data.
A catalogue record for this book is available from the British Library.

ISBN 978 0 7524 3639 5

Typesetting and origination by Tempus Publishing Limited
Printed and bound in Great Britain

Contents

The stage of the Tankerton Pavilion was the setting for this 1920s revue. The artists are unknown, but many stage shows involving the famous Jollity Boys were held in the marquee.

Acknowledgements

The majority of the old pictures come from my private collection, amassed over a period of twenty years, mainly through postcard dealers headed by Canterbury Postcard Club without whom my books would never have materialised.

I wish to thank the following for their photographic contributions and knowledge: Phillipa Tindall, R.M. Casserley (H.C. Casserley), Mike McWilliam – Silver Halide Photographers, Dennis Sharp – Ramsgate Motor Museum, Will and Brenda Austen, Judy Baker, as well as Seaward Colour Copy Shop for format alterations.

A special thank you to the photographers whose work appears, including Stephen and Douglas West, W.J. Cox & Sons, Rideouts and others, some of whom have remained unidentified. I have endeavoured to obtain permission to use material which may be under copyright and apologise for any omissions.

Additional information has come from Kent County Libraries of Canterbury and Whitstable. Many thanks to Manda Gifford at Whitstable museum concerning the 'Douglas West' collection and to the *Whitstable Times* newspaper for past advertising.

The preparation of the manuscript was undertaken by my daughter Lucy Glover and Joan Dobson; their help with this very time-consuming project was greatly appreciated.

Introduction

It was an honour to be asked to compile a follow-up book to *Whitstable* in the Archive Photograph series printed in 1998, and a privilege to accept the undertaking. However, the greatest motivation in producing this publication was the positive feedback and popularity of its predecessor.

Ancient records show that 'Northwood' was the first recorded name for Whitstable, which was on the route of a long distance footpath called the 'Saxon Shore Way'. Apparently the present name is made up of 'whit' meaning salt and 'stable' meaning market place. In Roman times the area would have been a mixture of marshland and forest terrain. The first sea defences date back to the fifteenth century but were periodically replaced as ineffective. Even modern sea-walls did not hold back the great floods of 1897, 1949 and the worst one in 1953.

The introduction of alleyways were used by the townsfolk as escape routes in their constant battles against the sea. Many stories involving these byways were told, maybe none more famous than the one about Feltham Alley between Middle Wall and Island Wall. Starting wide upon entry and bending in the middle, you would face a deceptive narrow exit of under two feet wide into Island Wall. Obviously this would have helped holding back a torrent of sea water for a while! It's present name of Squeeze Gut Alley possibly derives from the smugglers of the eighteenth and nineteenth centuries trying to escape capture from the pursuing excise man, but more probably from young lads being chased by the larger 'bobby' with the inevitable result – the sight is easy to imagine. The police force had arrived by 1857.

Assisted emigration to Australia by steamboat started in 1837 from this port, the population of which was around 3,000 people at this time. The 1850s heralded a building expansion programme between Oxford Street and Harbour Street, with the arrival of gas street-lighting. This busy fishing port and town was growing, resulting in a wealth of fish and seafood available. The oyster has been cultivated for over 2,000 years, with the world famous 'Native Oyster' closely associated with the town. Summer oyster festivals are now being celebrated every August.

Public transport started with the arrival of the first passenger train service in 1830, the old 'Crab and Winkle' line to Canterbury finally closing in 1952. The line can be partially followed along a footpath today. The London-Chatham-Dover line reached the town in 1860. Although the time of the journey to London then is unknown, in 1919 it was recorded as being one and a half hours by steam train, compared with only ten minutes less today by diesel electric – strange! The population had by now increased to around 8,000.

In mid-Victorian times public houses were at their most popular, reaching a peak of fifty in the area, compared with around thirty today. Restaurants and cafés however are now in abundance, highlighting the growth of the town in recent years. By 1970 the population had risen sharply to around 23,000. Today the population of Whitstable exceeds 30,000, with the town covering a total area of twelve square miles.

The most recent redevelopment 'The Horsebridge Project – Part 1' was finished in 2004; a shopping complex with an arts and community centre with galleries, a learning centre and performance space for music and variety shows over three levels. An old name for Whitstable, 'White Post' has appeared outside some living accommodation next to the centre, which is nice to see. The word Horsebridge comes from the jetty used in the past to collect catches from the boats.

Now join me in a walk through this most lovely of places, over a timescale of up to more than a century ago, and make your own comparisons with Whitstable today. It is an ever-changing society and one wonders what will happen in another 100 years – only time will tell!

Mick Glover
May 2005

Started by his grandfather, John Cox proudly stands in the doorway of the oldest-known family business in Whitstable, W.J. Cox & Sons. Once a quality printers, library and home to the *Whitstable Times* newspaper, it stands the test of time.

The Whitstable Pageant of 1910 was held in August. Groups of men, women and children represented a different country and the procession marched to Kingsdown Park. Although national costume was not compulsory, there can be no doubt that everybody did their best. Proceeds went into church funds and restoration work in parishes. Social activities at this time were organised by local churches, involving the town residents in many large-scale gatherings and competitions as well as the normal church services. It seems that for this picture the photographer forgot to say 'cheese'.

Chapter 1

The Journey Begins

Our journey begins near the top of Borstal Hill, approaching Whitstable as if travelling from the city of Canterbury. The windmill, probably originally called the 'Black Mill' when built around 1800, was apparently painted white up to 1885 and was later tarred black. With its four sails this old corn mill was one of three known working mills in Whitstable. Situated along today's Millers Court, from the late 1950s, redevelopment resulted in Whitstable's motel and restaurant arrival under the ownership of R.C. Harbourne, although Martin and Lesley Roberts also ran the business at one time. By 1973 Giovane and Noreen Ferrari had taken over the restaurant, which finally closed in 1987. The court is now filled with attractive modern houses and flats. Restricted access has resulted in today's view being taken from the other side.

Further down the hill we see the Four Horse Shoes public house in this ageless photograph. Established beside a blacksmith's forge around 1845, it was once called the Horseshoe Inn. This weather-boarded cottage was actually built some years previously. The inn was leased by the brewers W.E. & J. Rigden of Faversham and later sold to Percy Neame, another Faversham brewer. A local guide from the early 1900s remarks that the inn was 'much frequented by the modern mode of transport, the bicycle rider'. The cyclist coming from Canterbury would have welcomed this stop for refreshments after six miles. Today it is a Shepherd Neame establishment with Jane Geake the present landlady for nearly four years. The housing estate in the new picture can be clearly seen, with today's pub sign showing a bit more imagination than its predecessor.

View from Borstal Hill. Whitstable

Borstal Mill Whitstable

Reaching the bottom of the hill, we turn around and view the windmill and mill house, the original picture showing the peaceful scene in the 1920s. The mill once had a famous resident by the name of Henry Irving, an actor who purchased it in 1906, converting an upper room into a studio and setting up a lithograph press in the mill base. His brother Lawrence, also an actor, tragically lost his life by drowning with his wife when the *Empress of Ireland* foundered in the St Lawrence River in Canada on 29 May 1914. His son Captain Lawrence Irving was the owner of the mill in 1924 and wrote at least one book in the studio. During the Second World War the windmill was used as an army observation post. In the original photograph the left-hand pavement is non-existent, but was added later when houses appeared where the open spaces used to be, as in the up-to-date picture. The other side remains unchanged. Obviously motor cars were new on the scene with a motorist happily driving in the middle of the road not expecting to pas another.

Resuming our tour into Whitstable we come across the Tollgate, situated at the junction of Canterbury Road and Joy Lane off to the left in the direction of Seasalter. The original tollgate house, built in 1737, was by the junction of Canterbury Road and Oxford Street heading towards the main shopping centre. The toll for the Canterbury to Whitstable turnpike road, dating back to 1736, was abolished in 1871. J.T. Reeves & Son, who previously had offices in Oxford Street and High Street, occupied the house, as seen in this undated card. Nobody seemed to stay there any length of time, with other businesses such as tea-rooms and provision stores occupying the site up to the 1980s. Today it is a private residence. Along the front and to the right there used to be a horse trough standing there from 1896 presented by the actor Arthur Pinero and his wife. He also owned Tankerton Towers

(mentioned later) at one time. The trough was replaced in 1936 by the Metropolitan Drinking Fountain and Cattle Trough Association of London. It later became surplus to requirements and now holds bedding plants and bears a commemorative plaque. Memories come flooding back to me of the rag and bone man Les Tolputt's horse and cart stopping there before proceeding up Borstal Hill in the 1950s and '60s.

Travelling further down Canterbury Road this view is from around 1900, a time of gas lighting and the horse and cart. Local deliveries were reliant on this mode of transport and so stables were plentiful, just as the petrol filling station is today. Far left at No. 88 lived Mr Goldfinch, a builder, the house is still a private residence. Just out of the picture to the left and opposite the right-hand building is the Two Brewers public house, the area's oldest existing drinking house. The private houses between Nos 99–109 became shops later but did not fare too well. To the right we can see the trees are gone now and a housing estate built, the pavement thus being widened.

Further along the road we now come face to face with the Two Brewers Inn at No. 72. Despite the exteriors appearance changing over the years, the original brick structure has not changed in over 300 years. Originally a cottage in 1671, by around 1700 it had become an alehouse, an early innkeeper was Thomas Wright. Changing hands several times, by 1825 Rest Flint (later Flint & Co.) had purchased the pub. The forge opposite was once owned by Stephen Saddleton around 1858, also the pub licensee. Arthur Bertram, a London theatre manager, was licensee in 1923, and the 1930s picture shows him duly posing, a very interesting character and landlord for many years. Mrs Philippa Tindall has been licensee since December 1998 and this is a free house. Interestingly, the pub sign of today – just out of view – still shows two old characters in period clothes sharing a mug of ale.

Canterbury Road, Whitstable. 137494

Before going onto Oxford Street this quaint picture epitomises the peaceful and quieter way of life of the 1930s. To the left nearest the camera was G.E. Priestley's fish shop at No. 24. No. 18 was occupied by Law's household supplies, becoming Dillnot's the bakers by 1935. The garage sign indicates W.J. Maflin's Whitstable Motors, which traded from 1929 to 1963. Petrol was sold from National Benzole pumps close to the road; they were later set back for safety reasons and a new garage built. Now we have the Seven Seas fish restaurant, Michael Martin Partnership (accountants) with Alldays supermarket in a new building taking over the grounds of the garage. No. 43 to the right shows bicycles outside William Hayward's cycle shop, later taken over by his sons Reg and Geoff after the war until their retirements, a very successful and popular business. On the corner was Robin's Stores with W.T. Rising as proprietor at No. 41, in the foreground we have Miss Jackson's post office. Now they are the Four Seasons Chinese takeaway and a private residence, Hayward's at present is vacant. Apart from the loss of the garage and the inclusion of a signalled pedestrian crossing the architecture remains the same some seventy-five years later.

Heading towards the town centre, we stop at No. 43, 1910. Although the premises have become vacant, analysis of the word impressions left above the shop frontage shows that the baker William Fink was a previous occupier. He actually rented the shop from George Daniels Jnr between 1904 and 1910. His other premises were at No. 1 Harbour Street. The signboard says 'Pastry Cook W. FINK. Confectioner'. By 1914 No. 43 had been taken over by J. Powell a watchmaker, although no record of a polishing and furniture repair business, detailed on the front door, has been found. J.T. Reeves & Son estate agents mentioned earlier were at this time at No. 64 Oxford Street. From 1920 to 1987 it became the premises of Hayward's successful cycle shop. To the left would have been the grocer's shop of W.B. Nicholls, changing to G. Bakers grocery stores by 1911, advertised as selling Gilbey's wines and spirits. Now the cycle shop is empty with the takeaway at No. 41 to the left.

In the past, horse and carts would have been rattling along Oxford Street, as in this picture taken in 1910. The well dressed gentleman on the pavement is apparently reading a newspaper before perhaps catching a train at the station nearby. Miss A. Hales' tobacconists and confectionery shop was far left at No. 78, trading from 1910 until the late 1920s. Today the shop is Audrey's ladies hairdressers. The East Kent public house just out of sight beyond the man pictured dates back to around 1850 and is still a drinking establishment. On the corner of Cromwell Road to the right was Mrs C.A. Horden's china and glass shop at No. 55, which is now C.W. Lyons & Sons undertakers. The buildings have changed little in nearly a century.

This 1930s shop front to Nos 75 and 77 shows Ernest and Mary Wetherly's bakers shop with refreshment rooms out the back. They took over Mr W. Whitmore's bakery in 1923. His son Dennis and his wife Mavis took over the business, later relocating to No. 63 High Street until retiring in 1994. Many pharmacies occupied No. 73 to the left but probably Gillman and Clarke occupied the shop at the time of this picture. By the 1950s Graham Bowen's chemists had become the established name in pharmacy. Today the baker's shop is empty after being a launderette and the chemists have become Busy B's stores. The alleyway to the right once led to the St Alphage National Infants school, now relocated to No. 25 Oxford Street. The old railway station was also nearby, and a point of interest is that W.H. Smith stationers once had a newspaper stand there.

Oxford St. Whitstable.

Along the road a little, the large houses in view catered for the medical profession, with the dentist H.V. Stebbings on the corner at Cromwell House, Dr Callender next door at Garfield House, and the surgeon J. Hayward at Western House, later taken over by the dentist H.W. Dixon. Western House at No. 61 is today the headquarters of the Royal British Legion having moved in the 1980s from the former Forresters Hall, also in Oxford Street. The other two houses are now private. The card is dated 1935, the shop window furthest left is from the drapers shop of Hunnisett Brothers and Cromwell Road is off to the left. Today it is C.W. Lyons & Sons undertakers.

The well-advertised shop of
J. Mannooch – Oxford Street
stores is at No. 29 Oxford Street and
can be seen in this rare photograph.
Probably his son operated the handcart
used for local deliveries. The well-
stocked window fronts indicate a
range of groceries comparable to
today's small supermarkets. However,
I can well remember the time it took
to gather all the goods required on a
shopping list from a similar general
stores. The shop was open from
1901 to 1914 and remained a grocery
provisions store until at least the 1970s
with owners such as T. Brenchley,
J.T. Huson, Bourke & Hayes, C.J.W.
Bullen-Smith and The Mascot.
Looking similar today it is now the
premises of Paul Hammock's Angling
and Camping Centre for over three
years, with an employee only too
happy to pose for the camera.

completed for the grand opening on 27 July 1936. The film advertised, *Funny Face*, was shown later on in the year, a 1935 film from a United States version called *Bright Lights*. Very popular were the stills on show either side of the entrance. The placard (centre) shows a film yet to be seen, namely *She* starring Randolph Scott. The top of the drainpipes, still in evidence today, show the date 1936, the year of the cinema's inauguration. However, surprisingly the name is yet to appear. Despite a very successful and smart venue 'in the old days', a gradual deterioration in audience numbers forced eventual closure in 1984. The bingo craze took over and the building is still used as a bingo hall today, although many original features inside still remained upon my last visit

Proceeding further down the street and on course for the High Street, the Oxford cinema comes into view. It started life as the Oxford Animated Picture Hall in 1912, the owners being Maxfield & Day. This picture was taken after the original building was demolished and the new building

ot far to the right of the cinema stands the Seasalter Parish Hall. This photograph, taken at the outset of the First World War outside the hall, shows just one venue for the recruitment campaign. Others included the Palais-De-Luxe cinema, the Drill Hall in Cromwell Road and possibly the Horsebridge. These soldiers posing for the war effort, probably from the East Kent regiment 'The Buffs', cover a wide age spectrum, probably to entice as many men to join as possible. Inside the railings we see an older man, the recruiting officer, with his horse-drawn carriage. It was well-advertised with messages of 'Men of the Empire', 'Call to arms' and 'Your country needs you!' This followed Lord Kitchener's appeal for 100,000 volunteers. A 1919 official handbook states that over 700 men served from the town. Today, apart from the missing railings, the site remains the same.

artistic addition to the public buildings of the town', the Seasalter Parish Hall was opened on 25 April 1906, with the Revd T. Pitman MA as vicar in attendance. Magic lantern picture shows appeared there around 1910, the forerunner to main films being shown at the Oxford cinema opening in 1912 alongside. It was also frequently used for concerts and other entertainment as well as local functions. Today known as St Mary's Hall, it is home to the community centre previously at the Horsebridge (mentioned later). Various groups have access to the hall, including martial arts classes, and jumble sales and boot sales have also been held there. The entrance is the starting point for health walks. Downstairs is the Citizens Advice Bureau.

Built by late 1905 by Amos & Foad builders from a design by A.A. Kemp, an early stone was laid by Henry Western Plumptre and inscribed '22 November 1905'. Described later as 'a particularly

Taken from the corner of Argyle Road in the year 1900, this time-worn photograph shows to the right where the Parish Hall was to be shortly built. Although no record of a cycle shop can be found, as per the sign, today this shop at No. 10 is owned by Clark Building Contractors. While most of the properties on this side were private dwellings, the Oxford cinema would later appear just beyond the telegraph pole. Interestingly two old public houses next to the cinema could have been found there at one time, the Brewery Tap from 1856-1911 at No. 20, and the lesser-known King William 1855-1878 at No. 22. They are now the shop Best Book Deals and a private timber-framed house looking as it did 150 years ago. Mr A. Ganns, a shipowner was in residence at Melrose Villas at No. 12 in the foreground.

On the opposite side of the street we have a lovely view of shops now very much lost in time. The view was taken in 1922 with Walter Ford's hosier shop at No. 5 trading from the same year to 1934. The sale signs denoting 'After Season Sale of Surplus Stock' probably indicates that stock was taken over from the previous shopkeeper Mr C. Baker. The posh gentleman's outfitters Aubrey Pearce took over from Walter Ford's and was still listed in a local street directory in 1970. Today the shop is Beach Interiors. To the left would have been A.T. Pannell's piano and music shop and today it is Kites and Things at No. 3. At No. 7, Stanley Reeves' was a builders and decorators, today it is home to the Whitstable Visitors Centre. In between Nos 5-7, laid back, is the Forresters Hall dating back to the 1880s, the meeting place of the Ancient Order of Forresters, previously a schoolroom. More recently the British Legion was located there and this was the first meeting place of Whitstable Urban District Council. Since 1985 the Whitstable Heritage Museum has been located there.

Chapter 2

Town Centre

Concert parties were the order of the day from pre- to post-war days and the stage of the Argosy cinema was the setting for this orchestral concert party. Notice the radio microphone at the centre of the stage. Many musical revues involved servicemen who became quite accomplished for their time. Previously called the Picture House it became the Argosy on 13 February 1937, later renamed the Regal in 1953 until closure in 1960. The premises at Nos 44-48 High Street are now home to a Somerfield supermarket.

We are now in the town centre High Street but at the time of this very old photograph it was called Whitstable Street. This 1860 view shows the unmade road in a bad condition with much horse-drawn traffic using this thoroughfare. Fenn's watchmakers and clock shop at No. 65 was one of a few shops at this end of town that were combined with private residences. The shop became W. Holden's jewellers by the 1890s, occupying the premises till the late 1930s. Barclays Bank Ltd, in a restyled building, now occupies the site. The name Holden now appears at No. 84 on the opposite side of the road. The cottage on the left with steps and rails became the Salvation Army Citadel by 1886 but has now closed its doors and is at present vacant. Both the road and pavements would improve with time.

Going forward in time to around 1905, this would seem a very quiet time of day except for a man attending to his cart and a boy not wishing to pose for the photographer, perhaps needing to avoid horse dropping deposits. The Queen's Head Inn (to the right) is at No. 95. The first listed beer–retailer in 1845 was William Butcher. By 1871 it became known as 'Queen Anne's eating-house', later becoming the Queen's Head. Trade dropped off forcing closure in 1912. Today Pirie & Cavender's bookshop occupies the ground floor. The shop to the left was apparently the town's first bookshop during the 1860s, but by the 1900s it was H. Fagg's ironmongers shop at No. 93. At No. 91 was G. Daniels auctioneers and the M.O. & T.O. post office at No. 89. These properties are now Copperfield's general supplies,

Granny Smith's fruiterers and East Kent Model Shop. To the left at No. 98 was R. Woodland, a saddler. The shop with the canopy was Miss Harding's tea room at No. 90. No. 98 is now empty with Rob Smyth's clothes shop at No. 90.

This time-worn picture from around 1900 captures those days of horse-drawn conveyance with children going about their everyday lives. Shops were being established such as nearest the camera (left) I. Mitchell – tailor, W.F. Rigden's – fishmongers and, under the canopies, T. Coleman – domestic hardware, J. Rowden – fishmonger and Miss Kemp the greengrocer. To the right were G. Chambers – drapers, Jackson Brothers – tailors, D.J. Kemp – tobacconist and O. Holden – grocer. It is noticeable that shopkeepers at this time very much catered for the essentials in everyday life. The shops of today are covered in the next few pages, the most noticeable change being the replacement of upper floor bay windows.

The evening of Saturday 31 January 1953 finished with a breaching of the sea wall defences, which failed to hold back the inevitable torrent of sea water that drifted down to the High Street from Nelson Road. Fierce storms covered the South East resulting in severe flooding around the coast. The No. 4 bus from Canterbury appears to still be moving, unlike the motor car (probably an Austin 12) abandoned on the left and the bicycle which has been discarded to the right. At this time a new car would have set you back around £400. Behind the bus several cars including a Morris are queued up with nowhere to go. At No. 61 was the Maypole dairy 1928–late 1950s, with H.R. Butcher's bakery shop with a similar time period of trading. The Vitbe sign of No. 75 was in front of Peark's grocery shop which became Vye & Son. Today they are Staines' Farm Shop, Hubbard's bakery and Stuart's dry-cleaners.

Shadbolt's grocery shop. Alongside was Riceman's department store which later became Dawson's. All these shops started business soon after the end of the Second World War. Names such as HSBC Bank, Café Rio, Cousin's fish and chip shop, Stead and Simpson's clothes shop, Julian Graves' health food shop, Victoria Wines and R.J. Moore's opticians cover seven numbered properties. Across the road slightly obscured, Vye & Son grocery stores were situated in the forefront at No. 56, which is now Mackay's clothes shop. Woolley's shoe shop at No. 58 next to the bank was established in 1930 and is till open today. Shuttered shop fronts regretfully did little to stop water penetration – unlike the sandbags of today! Only slight development has taken place in the fifty years between these two pictures.

Not far from the last picture we see Greenstead & Son Ltd butchers shop on the left at No. 47 moving later to The Broadway in Swalecliffe. No. 49 was S.A.

A little further down the High Street, this picture was taken when the floodwater had begun receding. The boarded up shop to the left was Charlie Knowles' fruit shop at No. 39, with J.H. Dewhurst's the butchers at No. 41. No. 43 was the premises of R. Amos. Today we find the Rendez-vous coffee shop, Just Flowers and L.J. Bertram's jewellers shop. On the opposite side of the road in the forefront by the word 'THE' was the Regal cinema becoming Fine Fare supermarket in 1960. H.V. Davey furnishings was at No. 50 from 1920, E.A. Barton solicitors was at Nos 52–54. At the present time these are now the establishments of Whites of Kent and Furley Page solicitors.

What a charming scene captured for all time, showing residents of all ages pitching in to help clear away the snow following a blizzard in 1909. A horse and cart can be seen, over-laden of course. With the old Salvation Army building furthest left, next door was Baxter's confectionery shop at No. 72, today replaced by Card City. In the foreground to the right-hand side were bakers C.H. Holden and W. Dutfield's, a barbers and shaving establishment further down – notice the long barber's pole reaching into the road. The February 2005 photograph was taken following some of the worst snow that Whitstable had experienced in many years, although, to the photographer's annoyance, the snow flurries were dispersed too quickly. Nowadays hairdressing is continued by Identity, while the baker's is now a jeweller's called Ward & Corrigan.

Staying in the High Street this is a rare glimpse of three shops in the 1930s, showing that some businesses in the heart of the town seemed to enjoy a profitable time despite the general economic situation. Interestingly, some entertainers appear to be making a collection to ensure X-ray apparatus is purchased for the Whitstable and Tankerton hospital and gathering quite a crowd. The London Central Meat Company at No. 60 from 1904-1938, was owned by Mr Maynard. The well known and loved photographer Douglas West was in business with his father Stephen from 1919, taking over the family business in 1945 until his retirement in 1976. Stephen D. West previously had premises at No. 47 Oxford Street from 1914. At No. 68 was J. Scott & Son laundry and dyers from 1919-1960s, above can be seen the solicitors offices of Herbert William Guthrie. From left to right we now have the Hair Studio, Silver Halide photography, Woolwich Building Society and Clinton Cards.

As a complete contrast I have included a late 1960s view of a busy High Street on a lovely summer's day. This more up to date picture allows identification of shops to be made fairly easy. The Card Shop at No. 70, Mr Adam's clothes shop at No. 68, Douglas West, then Valente's coffee house and ice-cream shop at No. 64 in the 1960s and '70s with Currys electrical shop at Nos 60-62, Woolley's shoe shop at No. 58 and so on. The Regal cinema had already closed. To the right Dawson's department stores traded from the 1960s. Today's shops have been covered previously, but look very similar. The pedestrian crossing with the Belisha beacons is now traffic controlled. Unusually no vehicles are in view but for interest the national speed limit of 70mph was introduced in 1965 and the first self-service pump appeared in 1961.

Quite a busy scene in this early 1914 view showing the popularity of the motor car with open-topped and enclosed automobiles sharing the road with cyclists. I am reliably informed there is a bull-nosed Morris on the right. At Nos 57-59 we have C. Surman's butchers shop, which was located here from 1904 but moved to Tankerton in the 1960s. To the left was West's photographers shop and J. Scott & Son. The flags above the road indicate a forthcoming regatta day at the slopes of Tankerton. While new developments are now taking place to improve the town this area remains almost unaffected, as the up to date picture shows.

This 1929 picture reminds us of a time for motorists without parking restrictions applicable for the cars – even a truck has stopped in the middle of the road. There is also a car coming out of Gladstone Road to the right. Identification of the models is difficult from the rear, although Ford's were becoming popular at this time. The Toy Shop was owned by Misses E. and A. Chant at No. 72, now Card City. Next door was World Stores, which is now Gatesfield Sounds record shop. Surman's are still showing on the right, the building was built in 1928. Barclays Bank Ltd in the foreground was there from 1927 to the present day. The buildings on the left have been updated with a pedestrian crossing and road markings, non-existent all those years ago.

One of the great characters of the town was Charlie Knowles. Here we see him outside his greengrocer's shop at No. 39 in the 1920s, with produce from Covent Garden proudly advertised. What an abundance of quality fruit and vegetables on display. This wonderful picture captures a moment in time to be savoured. His father Edward Knowles started the family business in the 1890s, which became Knowles & Son by 1915. Charlie's sons Eric and Gordon joined later. Trading continued into the 1960s. Grandson Michael took the shop over as Michael's Salon, a ladies' hairdressers. He now owns Whitstable Nutrition Centre at No. 81. The building dates back to around 1880, and is at present called the Rendez-vous coffee shop.

Sunday school procession from around 1910, very popular at the turn of the century. Long-established businesses as seen in this view were the order of the day. In the forefront was T. Coleman, advertised as an oil and colour merchant, plus a domestic hardware store at No. 45 from the 1890s. At No. 43 was W.F. Rigden's, a fishmonger's from 1901 under the canopy, and W. & R. Fletcher's, a butcher's shop which traded from 1906 at No. 41. All three shops traded until the 1950s. At No. 39 was Knowles' and under another canopy was W.J. Cox & Sons stationers and printers, established in 1863, one of the longest running businesses in the town and still trading. HSBC Bank is now at No. 45 next door to the jeweller's and flower shops.

Heading towards the end of the High Street we come across a

They say every picture tells a story and this one is no exception. Taken at the turn of the twentieth century this lovely view shows three famous public houses with accommodation, standing in very close proximity with each other, a rarity even in those days. The Royal Naval Reserve, originally called The Rose from the 1840s, changed its name in 1876. Still very popular, the present licensee for over ten years is Mrs Sheila Luke. The Duke of Cumberland Hotel dating back to 1748, rebuilt after the fire of 1866, was modernised in 1900. Again very popular, winning an award for most improved pub of the year 2004, the present licensee for over two years is Mr Paul Guilfoyle. Both are Shepherd Neame houses. To the right with the bear sign was the Bear and Key Hotel, which operated under that name from 1739, a grand Georgian façade appearing in the late eighteenth century, updated in the 1870s. Regrettably closure was effective a few years ago. Briefly resurrected as Sherrin's by February 2001, final closure took place in October 2002. Many residents hope a drinking house will prevail at this site in the future.

A wonderful close-up view of the Bear and Key Hotel taken in the 1920s. Originally called The Ship in 1703, the first licensee was apparently John Hampton. In 1739 a new licensee, William Hogsflesh, changed the name and the establishment grew in stature over the next 200 years becoming one of the most popular drinking and eating establishments in the area. Pub outings and bus service trips commenced from this pick-up point. A second original doorway stood where the second window from the left is situated. The archway to the right originally led to stables and coach houses, but in more recent years led to a car park with restaurant and entertainment rooms upstairs. Sadly today's picture of this very impressive structure all boarded up is perhaps a sign of the times, and the colourful history of this pub deserves better. Partly obscured furthest left is No. 33 Harbour Street. At this time it was home to W.C. Humphrey's leather goods shop, which operated from the 1890s to the 1930s, later to become Boulting's fishing tackle shop, as I am sure many readers will remember. Now it is Marion Clement's clothes shop.

These last two exquisite postcards (this page and overleaf), taken at The Cross at the turn of the century, beautifully show life in Edwardian times. In the distance a handcart is left unattended while on the right is a delivery man with his horse and cart. Six public houses covered this end of the town. Sited with three long upper floor windows to the left just after the clothing sign was the Prince of Wales public house at No. 13, 1863-1967. A little further down was the Shades public house from 1878-1906, with the Hoy Endeavour Inn at No. 21, 1845-1906. Not long after this picture was taken these two inns were pulled down and rebuilt. Today the Job Centre, Alan R. Long butchers and Sense charity shop occupy the pubs' space. The Royal Naval Reserve is on the right with the Duke and The Bear back the other way. H.C. Solley's glass shop is shown left at No. 7 which is now Warrener's sports and leisure shop.

23450 Whitstable. High Street looking West.

A similar view a bit further along the road shows handcarts and horse and carts once again dominating the road space as people felt as safe there as on the pavement with the fairly slow pace of the time. The Edwardian style of dress in Whitstable is well captured on camera. Nearest to the camera on the right was Miss Walker's sweet shop at No. 10 and M.F. Spratt's haircutting salon at No. 12. Next door was the Capital and Counties Bank, the printing works frontage of No. 18 shows G. Joiner's stationers shop, Freeman Hardy & Willis shoe shop is further down the road, and after closure became a charity shop. In today's picture Kent Estate Agents, Lloyds Bank and Rayner's opticians now occupy the above premises. To the left, as advertised, was T. Staniland's outfitters shop until 1903, which became Hatchard's who recently celebrated their centenary and are still going strong.

Chapter 3

Horsebridge and One-Way System

Although people of the town worked very hard just to make a living, they also believed in taking their social lives very seriously. This photograph shows the 'Besses o' th' Barn Band', just one of the many brass orchestras that toured the country. They visited Whitstable for an open-air concert in 1930, though the actual venue is undetermined. If their musical performance matched their costumes then it would have been a very impressive show.

Before proceeding let us look at a popular yearly event. This is a 1920s carnival float with an oriental flavour proceeding along Cromwell Road, sponsored by Harold Wilman's furnishers shop based at Nos 107–109 High Street between 1915 and 1932. Foad's yard is on the left. In those days the floats were often horse-drawn with motor vehicles being few and far between. The carnivals, which were often held on a Wednesday, included confetti battles between participants and spectators alike and were very popular. Beauty contests meant that Miss Whitstable entered the affray along with other neighbourhood representatives. The contestants, I believe, would have been in the age group of late teens into their twenties. Here we also see the Miss Whitstable float of 2004, shown by kind permission of Mike McWilliam of Silver Halide Photographers, just one of many carnival queen floats. In recent years the participants have been around early teenage years. The beauty queen is Miss Siân Sidders aged thirteen to the left, with her deputy queen Danielle Cuttress and princesses Heidi Roberts and Rhiannon Champs in attendance. Businesses are often represented, with dancing groups, acrobats, bands and entertainers among the many entries. Proceeds, as ever, go to charity.

We venture on and this picture, although taken a few years ago, shows the Assembly Rooms at the Horsebridge, renamed the Re-assembly Rooms. Built by Thomas George Browning in 1868, the rooms were used for all manner of events including a music hall, orchestral concerts, variety shows and plays. There was also a library and many council meetings were held there. The first ever cinematograph shows in the town started there in 1908 in the Bioscope Theatre but with the arrival of other cinemas closure was effective by 1910. Johnny's Arthouse next door was T.W. Mitchell's furniture showrooms previously, with supermarkets such as Victor Values and Tesco once occupying this stretch. Demolition of the whole area took place during 2002 and the latest development to the town resulted in

new shops opening by 2004 with the Arts and Community Centre at the end of the building opening on 10 April 2004. Exhibitions and functions now take place there and the arrival of a film club showing alternative and foreign films brings the cinema appropriately back to its birthplace.

At the end of the Horsebridge, this early 1920s card shows an old Whitstable to Canterbury solid tyre bus – the lack of comfort for the passengers we can only imagine. To the left trips were well advertised from this starting point. The Whitstable Pure Ice Works were recorded as being in business from 1914-1923, with the Oyster Fishery Company to the right being their largest customer. Mr George Warner was manager and the business was later transferred to Canterbury. The Ice Works became public baths and later public conveniences before demolition in 2002 to make way for a new development. The Pearson's Arms public house dating back to 1840 hides beyond the factory and has since become as popular as ever as a seafood restaurant and bar now called the Pearson's Crab and Oyster House.

This interesting 1930s view shows the oyster packers at work, with many men employed by the Seasalter and Ham Oyster Fishery Company. Note the many stacks of empty baskets upstairs. The barrels also took care of the seating arrangements. Situated opposite the Pearson's Arms, the area has now become the Whitstable Oyster Company's very popular seafood restaurant at the Horsesbridge.

At the end of the High Street we venture into Harbour Street. This rare photograph showing the Hippodrome – presumably an early name for the Palais-De-Luxe cinema, designed by W.G. Sprague – is the only known picture of the cinema frontage. Starting in 1911 the canopied premises of No. 38 next door was added in 1921. Closure took place in 1931 with the end of the silents. It is now a shopping arcade with no reminder of it's interesting past. Next door from the 1890s was Ridout's stationers and printers, moving to Herne Bay by the 1960s. It was also a post office, library and newsagent's and is now Shapla Tandoori restaurant. To the left at No. 32 was W. Philpin the chemist's which became Walker & Harris from 1915, and is now Carole Ridley's clothes shop.

This similar view taken in 1907 shows the inactivity that enabled children to walk and play on the road or on the pavement without risk, along this one-way street. Philpin's chemist shop at No. 32 opened in 1904 and closed by 1914. Valentine's Stores at No. 31 became Edwin Chinnick's sweet shop in 1920, now Antoniou's Hair and Beauty Salon. Chinnick was later a manager of the Palais-De-Luxe cinema opposite. On the other side F.A. Boulding had a butcher's shop from 1901 to 1908. On the corner was E.P. Coleman's post office at No. 39. These are now Birdies restaurant and The Clothes Horse. Facing at No. 48 was O. Holden's Harbour Street stores, now the Williams and Brown tapas restaurant. The sign on the wall beyond is for the Nelson Inn.

A. Parsons was the manager. The pub traded from 1860-1981. In recent times it became council offices but is now empty.

an Austin and Morris in view and the road looking brand new. Petrol was 1s 6d per gallon at this time. Davey's house furnishings occupied Nos 37–38 from 1931, moving in the late 1950s to Foad's shop. Hector Davey also took over the Palais cinema premises at No. 43. Opposite at No. 31 from 1933 to the 1950s was Cyco-Radio Ltd wireless engineers. In the forefront was H.W. Gambell's sweet shop, H. Reeves' tearooms and the premises of the tailors Mr Pollock and Mr Camburn. The shopping arcade has replaced Davey's and Foad's has given way to Harbour newsagent's. To the right we now have Antoniou's Hair and Beauty salon, Mosaic, Tudor tearooms and Graham Greene's general store. The only other difference between the two views is the modernisation of the motor cars.

This is a 1934 view down Harbour Street looking towards the town centre. Ozzie Foad's cycle shop at No. 45, furthest left, began in the 1890s and with Mrs G. Foad he went on to repair vehicles till the 1960s. Cars were catching on at this time, with

Going on we view Harbour Street looking back from Ludgate Hill, dubbed 'Starvation Point'. Many businesses occupied these shops over the years including S. Philpott's outfitters, J. Lawson the house agent, E. Stutely dining rooms, the shipping industry represented by W.J. Lawson and J.R. Daniels and eating houses such as Mrs J. Anstiss' and W. Fowler's. Even my father ran an ice-cream parlour here in the 1940s. The South Eastern public house, popular with railway passengers, occupied a middle premises from 1867-1927. By the 1950s shops were being boarded up and the subsequent demolition and site clearance by the 1970s enabled a new landscaping project to be finished by 1989. The harbour entrance is opposite (just out of shot). The castellated building facing was erected in 1905. Wallace Pring, a dressmaker, occupied No. 1 in 1912, and a nice touch is the re-introduction of the name in recent times to this building.

This very rare 1910 photograph shows the rear of No. 1 Harbour Street in the one-way system. William J. Fink proudly stands to the left, his sons and helpers pose accordingly – the family resemblance is amazing. He ran the baker's shop from 1902 to 1920, the business being called Fink & Sons from 1915. No further information has come to hand after 1920 but probably the First World War contributed to the firm's demise. Interestingly the over-laden wagon filled with bread rolls seems about to topple over, with the handcart as a backup. From the 1880s to the 1960s the premises remained a baker's shop but became Bolton's newsagent by 1970. Today it is Wallace Pring's clothes shop. Ludgate Hill's Starvation Point shops can be seen in the distance.

Along Sea Wall there were many weather-boarded fisherman's cottages, some have remained, some have been modernised, while others have been demolished and rebuilt in conventional brickwork. They stretch all the way from the Horsebridge to the old Ludgate Hill. This undated card, probably from the 1960s, shows from farthest away: The Cottage, Seaview House and Estuary House, home of the Whitstable & District Angling Society. The nearest cottages are not recognisable today, either no longer there or rebuilt. Most of the houses have nautical names. Just beyond in the distance is Reeves Beach.

OLD FISHERMANS COTTAGES, WHITSTABLE

A GLIMPSE OF WHITSTABLE.

From a 1920s card this is a pleasant view onto Reeves Beach along Sea Wall, a popular walkway and resting place for the holidaymaker and residents alike. The beach is named after William Reeves, who in 1793 had a block and mast-making business opposite, ancestor to George Reeves who built an oval roller skating rink there after 1915, used till the late 1930s. History says that the first sea wall was built in 1583, the present sea wall was built in 1952 and the latest scheme, raising the beach, was in 1989. The first cottage is actually named The Cottage. Except for the removal of the gas lamp and the introduction of better seating arrangements, today's view is similar with the same pleasures being enjoyed at this location.

Chapter 4

Approaching Tankerton

Amusement arcades, always popular in seaside resorts, are represented in this time-worn picture of my grandparents William and Emma Glover's Tower Amusements at 1a Tower Parade. This interior view shows the sizes of machines available in the 1930s, including early cranes and pinball games. Opening in 1931 it successfully ran until retirement resulted in its closure by 1960. I wonder how many people like myself remember spending time and having fun here while losing their pennies. On the other side of the road would have been Jacque's arcade – the area was very popular with holidaymakers for its cafés, gift shops and of course early arcades. Today the games and machines may be more technologically advanced but their popularity has never waned for children and adults alike.

Taken outside the arcade this 1935 view is a family moment captured in time. Furthest right my uncle William Akhurst is standing alongside his parents Emma Jane and George William Akhurst. Mrs Akhurst, as we can see here, helped in the arcade. Today the premises have been completely modernised and are now Newmark pharmacy. Along the side was Edward Wood's fruit stores trading from 1935 to the 1970s and today this is known as The Garden Shop. At No. 2 was W.G. Ferneley's post office and general stores, open from 1921 to the 1960s, now New World Chinese takeaway restaurant.

Moving further along we now have a most exquisite 1905 postcard of the Memorial Fountain, which takes pride of place along the then Tankerton Terrace. It was probably erected in 1897 to commemorate Queen Victoria's Diamond Jubilee, but had gone by the 1920s. The faded inscription has been translated into a plausible but only possible reading:

ERECTED
Erected by inhabitants of Whitstable and Seasalter a commemorate of the completion of the sixtieth year of the happy reign of Her Majesty Queen Victoria 20th June 1897. Her court waits for her like servants. God gave her peace, her land... A thousand claims to reverence charged in her as mother, wife and Queen.

This view also shows the shop fronts of Daniels & Collar, a fancy goods shop, at No. 5, and C. Goldfinch's greengrocers at No. 6. A private house and INI Skateboard Supplies now occupy the old shops.

Further along to the left we now look at a 1930 picture revealing Mrs Bolton's stationers and ladies' salon business, recorded as trading up to 1932 at No. 6 Tower Parade. The name change appeared in 1925, and a reverse number change occurred in 1921. There is definitely a well-stocked shop window display to entice customers into the shop. To the left at No. 7 was Wells & Evans domestic goods shop that traded from 1926 well into the 1950s. Today's view remains similar with many of these old shops now becoming private residences. The shrubbed area appears well looked after in both pictures.

Away from the line of shops this view from around 1905 shows a castellated mansion called Tankerton Tower (known as The Towers) which has stood proudly as a well-known landmark since 1792. The land can be traced back to the thirteenth century when a knight called William de Tangreton is mentioned. Situated by Tower Parade it was added to in the 1830s by famous resident Wynn Ellis, who became known as 'Lord of the Manor'. The regatta once held there was transferred to Tankerton Slopes. He used the residence until his death in the 1870s. In more recent times concerts and dances were held in the grounds, with a bowling green opening in 1936. The gardens opened to the public in 1948 with the council purchasing the castle and grounds earlier. Today as a private residence the grounds remain open for all to walk through, sit down and admire. For a brief time in the early 1900s messages on postcards were written on the photo side but this idea was soon phased out.

Tankerton Tower, Whitstable.

D. A. H.
I hope you will like this P. C. of Tankerton I. A. M. bought me some p.c. I am sending one to Pat that I bough. The men make a nice noise only we miss it niedly in Barn from your loving neice H. m. s.

This 1910s view of Tankerton Terrace shows the shops of S. & E. Kemp drapers at No. 4, South Tankerton estate office at No. 3 and Miss E. Priors' stationers at No. 2. In the far distance we see the entrance-way to The Towers. Facing the camera was the Tankerton bakery of P. Smith's at No. 2 Tankerton Road. Shrub borders to the left made way for railings later, the memorial fountain can be seen far left. Now Smith's has become Budget Suite house clearances and the shops are private residences. No. 1 on the corner used to be the Tankerton stores of C. Coleman but alas today is a rundown ex-business.

This early 1880s view somewhat faded with time is looking towards Tankerton Terrace in the far distance. The Steam Packet Inn, a weather-boarded property, opened in 1836 and was popularly used by railway passengers from the station nearby. Burnt down in 1913 this was reconstructed in brick. It closed in 1962 and with the building next door became the premises of the Harbour Master, on the right, and customs office. The other side is yet to be developed. The Gorrell Reservoir was concreted over in the 1970s. Pavements were yet to appear. The 'Crab and Winkle Line' ran across the road further down to the harbour. The Steam Packet now plays host to the Whitstable & District Angling Society.

In today's view the customs office no longer stands, with traffic lights in place to control the intersection with Cromwell Road to the right.

Heading towards the sea this is a 1940s view of Beach Walk. The popular swing-boats on the beach were erected in the 1890s but were pulled down after the 1953 flood. The Continental Hotel shown on the left of the buildings dates back to 1890 and was at one time called Harbour Lights. Originally two buildings, one a café the other called Beulah, it gradually became one and was renamed the Continental. Now the downstairs is a bar and restaurant, the upstairs hotel section is flats. The other buildings included the Kiosk – an ice-cream and mineral shop – Rybar Laboratories and the Sisters Café with Dadd's gift shop and arcade just out of picture. Today they are mainly residential. Interestingly the other end of Beach Walk now holds Whitstable Windsurfing and Water Ski Club (a placard outside says 'Whitstable World Champions'). The building by the swing-boats held public toilets downstairs, as today, although the seating area upstairs has since been boarded up.

oing back in time this view was taken from a similar standpoint n a blustery winter's day in the 1910s : Tankerton Beach. The path in the istance leads to the slopes, usually very pleasant walk. Being out of ason the swing-boats are of course ot in action. Londoners coming own by train treated Whitstable a health spa during the summer onths. Apart from a house and some halets, the area was yet to be built up. he recent picture shows a modern uilding to the right and the public uilding mentioned previously to the ft.

We can now journey on to Tankerton and going down Tankerton slopes towards the sea we view a stretch of land called 'The Street', in this postcard marked 1914. This was a bank of shingles visible at low tide that can go out from three quarters of a mile to over a mile and originally called 'Street Stones'. Many people have enjoyed a pleasant walk here and can collect shellfish along the way caught in the many pools of water left behind. Guests from the nearby Tankerton Hotel would include this interesting walk in their stay, copying local residents and holidaymakers alike. Today nothing has changed, even the beach huts remain but have of course been added to.

Further along the beach this Edwardian picture shows the Whitstable Regatta – an important event to look forward to for all the residents. This started in 1792, with the boating taking pride of place. Many people would watch sailing boat races from their viewpoint on the slopes (comfort did not seem to matter in those days at all). The ladies look very elegant in their long dresses. Punch and Judy shows could be seen every year along the top. Today the Regatta, usually held in July, is largely held on the top of the slopes with sideshows being very popular indeed. Today's picture shows a much quieter scene taken in the month of February with large beach huts that run right the way along the slopes.

Tankerton, Aug 25th 1910, Regatta – Day.

In this 1946 postcard, there is a lot of activity along the slopes. The bandstand to the right was built around 1910 and hosted many recitals – especially on Regatta day – with various Whitstable bands playing there. It was pulled down in the 1940s. The Tankerton Hotel was situated at the top of the hill and started trading in 1902. By the 1950s only the bar downstairs, renamed the Tankerton Arms, was open and the hotel rooms had been converted into flats. This is now a private residence. The public convenience building to the left was later moved to Marine Parade further down the road but a seating area now stands on this site.

The dawn of the twentieth century was to shortly inspire redevelopment in Tankerton. Cliff Terrace to the right became Marine Parade with the Marine Hotel having been constructed in the 1890s. Tankerton Estate was being developed with the main road to the right being built in 1920. Walks at the top of the slopes became popular necessitating seating areas as shown in this view. Today's picture is dominated by housing going all the way up the hill and the ever-present motor cars taking up the car parking spaces along the road. The somewhat uneven track in the old picture has long gone with a grass way making a more pleasant area.

Towards the end of Marine Parade used to be the Tankerton pier, constructed in 1894 by Homan & Rogers for £660. Sited opposite was the Royal Hotel. The walkway for access to boats can be clearly seen. Nicknamed 'the Bedstead' because of its structure, the pier fell into disuse and was dismantled by George Warner in 1913. A point of interest is that the wooden steps up Tankerton Slopes from the pier were replaced by fifty-seven large concrete steps, presumably for safety reasons. The road at the top of the slopes was originally called Station Road, when the railway station was supposed to have been built locally at Ham Shades Lane. This did not happen and redevelopment of the road resulted in a new name of Pier Avenue in 1903.

Situated alongside the Marine Hotel 'The Troc' cinema opened on 9 February 1931 with entrance through Tankerton Grand Pavilion, built in the late 1920s from a design by Major W. Puttich. Originally it was a roller-skating rink. The film advertised, *Whoopee*, was one of the first films to be shown there. The commissionaire in his peaked cap was a Mr Dowdy who can be seen by the entrance to the Pavilion. Until recently the metal supports for the word cinema were very much in evidence. Owned by George Fitt the full capacity was around 1,500 seats, including a small circle upstairs of 250 seats. This posh venue closed its doors in the early 1950s. Used for several purposes, deterioration resulted in the building at the rear being vacant for a long time. The building was demolished in 1996 and the area remains vacant. The Pavilion is completely residential now. An Austin 7 on the left has been identified.

This 1932 view along Marine Parade esplanade shows the Marine Hotel to the left. Originally a terrace block of four large houses they were developed by the Tankerton Estate Co. and completed in 1895. Mr George Fitt purchased the property and converted part of it in 1906 and fully established the Marine in 1926. Notice the name TROC on the elevation above the word 'CINEMA' for the venue. The Troc Bazaar advertised was run by Mrs Dowsett but operated for only two years from the opening of the cinema. You will notice the various open- and closed-top motor cars all along the road and even a van. Recognising the makes of cars offers an interesting challenge to the reader.

Chapter 5

The Railway Influence

Public transport, such an important part of our national heritage, is covered in the next few pictures regarding the introduction of the train. The Whitstable to Canterbury railway was opened on 3 May 1830, the first railway to employ steam power in southern England and the first steam-hauled passenger service in the world. The six-mile journey was covered by a locomotive engine for the first two miles with the last four miles operated by stationary steam winding engines. The very first locomotive was the old *Invicta* based on George Stephenson's famous *Rocket*. His son Robert undertook trial runs on the 2 May 1830 with the first journey undertaken on that famous day, 3 May 1830. Taken from two engravings this would have been the return journey from Whitstable, the viewpoint probably from the top of All Saints church with the town of Whitstable in the background and the Isle of Sheppey beyond. High maintenance costs for the next twenty-odd years resulted in the Canterbury and Whitstable Railway Co. being dissolved by the end of 1853 and the South Eastern Railway was then born. Affectionately called the 'Crab and Winkle' line the quicker access to the city of Canterbury must have opened up a complete new world to local residents. Regretably the remainder of the nineteenth century is not too well documented, although we do know that improved locomotives followed the *Invicta*.

but became ineffective by 1836 and was withdrawn from service shortly afterwards. This was not the end of the road though for this locomotive, which appeared in many exhibitions including Stockton in 1925. It later reached this resting place by the city wall outside the Dane John gardens in Canterbury until deterioration resulted in restoration work by the Transport Trust and the engine being kept undercover inside a museum. The present view had to be taken with the round turret on the wall appearing on the right as reconstruction work now being undertaken would have meant the same picture showing a lot of scaffolding and thus an ineffectual picture. The medieval defence wall followed the same line as its predecessor.

George Stephenson's locomotive *Invicta* was used on the Whitstable to Canterbury line from 1830

Taken at the old railway station by the harbour this picture postcard printed in 1980 affectionately shows the glory of the steam age with this South Eastern Railway train. Mr Casserley's son tells me that the train was an R class A124, with mixed carriages of the new Southern Railway stock. The train was apparently the 12.10 to Canterbury travelling on Saturday 6 August 1927. With the motor bus becoming increasingly popular on the roads, the last passenger service on this line was in December 1930. The freight train continued however, until this service was also finished on 29 November 1952. The removal of the complete seven mile railway line was undertaken during 1953. This was the end of a glorious era. Today's view was taken on Easter Friday with the Victoria to Thanet diesel electric train arriving at the present Whitstable station at 3.05 in the afternoon. The number on the rear of the train, 375601, apparently indicates the line and train number.

At the top of Ludgate Hill you would have ventured through the harbour gates in the 1900s and seen this delightful view of the harbour. This lad together with the men to side seemed to be enjoying the view of the boats in the harbour. Coal wagons can be seen on the railway sideline that would have been on course to Canterbury and many goods were transported by this method. The tall chimney seen in the background was for the overworked coke ovens that have long since vanished. Today in place of the railway line there is a seafood shop and restaurant, with many buildings in the space, going the other way, including the Royal National Lifeboat Institute. The entire area has become very popular for residents and tourists alike and seems very busy.

The old Whitstable to Canterbury railway station by the harbour of the 1880s shows staff happily posing both on the platform and on the line – no fast-moving express trains for them to be wary of. Today the Whitstable Health Centre together with the county council's youth club built in 1970 dominates the site of the old railway station with no evidence remaining of any of the old buildings.

We now leave the area and venture onto the present Whitstable railway station. This 1950s picture shows the platform to the station on the Old Bridge Road side. From this we can see to the right a weighing machine with a self-service chocolate machine beside it, but these have disappeared A long queue of school children, towels in hand, are possibly waiting to go home following a swim in the sea. Perhaps the reader can identify a face or two? The train is no longer as popular as it used to be and local stations like Whitstable reflect this in their emptiness and lack of services. Even the newspaper stand inside by the ticket office is no longer there and in comparison with years ago the station is now just functional.

Upon leaving the station this undated card shows a placard which is self-explanatory. Situated opposite along Old Bridge Road one cannot help but wonder whether permission had been granted for this rather elaborate message to be erected. At least one young ladies attention has been drawn to it, her dress indicates that this photograph was possibly taken in the 1950s. A paying car park available for the railway traveller now adorns this site.

FOR THE WAGES OF SIN IS DEATH. THE GIFT OF GOD IS ETERNAL LIFE

SIN PAYS WAGES

GOD GIVES LIFE

OLDEST RAILWAY BRIDGE IN THE WORLD, TANKERTON   H 6870

This bridge at the bottom of the Bridge Approach coming down to Old Bridge Road by the railway station was, wrongfully in the opinion of the majority of residents, demolished in 1969. Constructed in the late 1820s for the Whitstable to Canterbury railway line, the powers that be had decided that with its renowned 'blind spot' it was too dangerous for the ever increasing volume of traffic on the roads. An Armstrong Siddeley, I believe, is approaching. It makes you wonder how many of the motorists who had the privilege to negotiate this piece of road over the years are glad the bridge was removed. Not many I bet.

Chapter 6

Out and About

One of the many side roads in Whitstable is Warwick Road where Stanley Reeves Ltd had a builders' yard and this view shows the aftermath of an arsonist at work on the night of 21 September 1932. The national newspapers recorded by 9 November that year that three major fires had taken place, the other two being a restaurant in an undisclosed location and a timber yard in Cromwell Road. Whitstable and Herne Bay fire brigades tackled the blazes and at the time it was reported that the perpetrator was still at large.

A walkabout around Whitstable could not leave out a walk along West End Beach heading towards the Neptune public house. The Old Neptune dates back to 1852, when the original building, a boat building shop, was swept away in 1898 and rebuilt to its present wooden construction using material from ruined cottages nearby. There have been many licensees, including the very first, Harry Keam, who remained for over forty years. Mrs Phoebe Ramsley was in charge during the 1938 and 1953 floods. In this old Whitbread house today's present licensees are Keith Flynn and Darren Wilton who from 2002 proudly continue this proud heritage (opposite, below). Very popular, especially in the summer months with the tourist industry, the pub defies the tides year in, year out, and one wonders whether there are other pubs in the country standing on a beach. This 1911 dated card (above) shows a very crowded beach with sunbathers and swimmers alike arriving at this period in time in formal clothing. Bathing huts in view could be rented for the day as changing rooms, the canvas coverings meaning no locked doors and they were available for most times of the year. Beyond the terraced houses there were tennis courts, as today. The only difference with the modern view (opposite, above) is that fewer people nowadays seem to take advantage of the simple pleasures in life.

Looking back the other way we view terraced houses along Wave Crest and these were used mainly as holiday apartments. The walkway was later widened to accommodate access by motor car. This time-worn photograph, probably taken in the 1910s shows two ladies enjoying the view on a warm summer day, but where are the sun worshipers? Perhaps it was too early in the day! On the beach was the schooner *Vigilant* which was used as a training ship but has long since disappeared.

This postcard of Dick Scammell's very popular boating lake along West Beach Road must bring back a lot of memories to any child that visited and gained a lot of pleasure there. Situated by the golf course, a dyke was developed into the lake. The author remembers rowing boats, paddles and canoes ever available for a time period of twenty minutes, with a call of 'your time is up' by a man pointing at you to come in. Tracing back to the 1920s other activities available there were putting and crazy golf with amusements in the café entrance at the front. By the 1980s popularity had dwindled with the Squash Racket Club building taking its place until the 1990s relocating to Beach Walk, the lake by this time being filled in. The site as we can see today has been redeveloped and is now part of a modern housing estate.

An interesting side road is Westcliffe Road, just off Nelson Road from Oxford Street. This photograph shows No. 39 in the foreground which was Westfields nursing home. In this timeless photograph, opposite but out of view, is the Whitstable and Seasalter Golf Course formed in 1909, advertised then as a nine hole course with a green fee of 2s 6d per day. This backed onto Dick Scammell's boating lake. Most of the houses in today's view, with little change, are residential, although there is now a nursing home at Nos 27 and 28.

This side road called Island Wall shows the floods of 1953, the flood water very high at this time was taken on 1 February, this road running in close proximity, parallel to the sea wall. The houses were actually lower than the usual sea level. The depth of the water can be seen by the car in view. The corner shop at No. 15 by Beach Alley was owned by H. Williams by 1957, as recorded in a local street directory, and previously was William Rollinson's grocery shop after the war. The owners can be seen at the top windows wondering perhaps whether help would ever come! Further down the road was the Guinea public house at No. 31 occupied by R.L. Gamble. Open in 1861 it had a good reputation for entertainment and outings but nevertheless Whitbread closed the inn in 1981. Today they are both private houses with No. 15 being modernised. Just beyond the corner shop was William Tilley's, a fried fish dealer, and the Whitstable Urban District Council's store yard. These and other buildings were demolished in the 1960s with redevelopment resulting in new houses being built, as can be seen in today's view.

Should we proceed down Joy Lane we reach Seasalter. Postmarked 1936 this picture postcard shows the Crossways, now known as Seasalter Cross, signposted Hernhill, Faversham and Whitstable. Interestingly the two mile signpost to Whitstable ends at the Horsebridge. The reason for this is unknown, but possibly because organised outings started off at the Bear and Key Hotel nearby or from the Horsebridge, focal points of the community. Today the signpost points to Canterbury, Seasalter and Whitstable, the change possibly due to these being more central locations. Redevelopment has resulted in housing estates popping up all around this area.

Continuing onto the Faversham road, this 1930s view shows the Parade, which was an uneven unmade track before the road was widened and built up properly. Interestingly the remains of thirteenth-century salt workings were found in 1955 close to the sea by archaeologists, confirming the origin of the name 'Seasalter'. The beach has now been properly cordoned off with the road that eventually leads to Ye Olde Sportsman public house. It is so nice to see these old 1920s motor cars, such as this Austin, in view.

SHAFTESBURY SOCIETY'S HOSTEL, SEASALTER

building from 1927 as a holiday home for deprived children from the London area. The Society had purchased surrounding land earlier in 1920. There were up to 100 boys and girls staying there at any one time. Originally constructed in 1873 it became known as 'the Battery' and was used by the Navy. During the First World War it was used by the armed forces as a convalescent home and during the Second World War it was also used by the British Army. After 1946 it once again became a holiday home for children for a while before deterioration resulted in it being pulled down. Now no longer there, the newer building in view is the headquarters to the Seasalter Water Ski Club.

Further along the Faversham road and just off the beach, the Shaftesbury Society, a volunteer group of people, used this wooden

Travelling along the road we now come to Ye Olde Sportsman public house at the end of Seasalter in the 1920s. An interesting story has been told in the past of a German Junkers 88 bomber coming down during the Battle of Britain on 27 September 1940, landing nearby, with a group of Irish soldiers rushing from the inn fighting with the crew until they surrendered. An episode from the television series *Dad's Army* was based on the story. The inn began its life in 1814 and was caught up in smuggling in the nineteenth century. To the side the picture also shows an ice-cream and mineral kiosk, presumably to keep the children happy. At the front an Austin 7 is parked. The current view is unfortunately obscured with trees and undergrowth but nevertheless still looks as impressive as ever. It is a Shepherd Neame house, and the present licensee Philip Harris has been resident for over five years.

Johns Road, Swalecliffe. This road in fact leads to Colewood Road on the way to Herne Bay. The road to the right goes off to Goodwin Avenue. Regrettably, despite exhaustive enquiries, the author has been unable to identify the owners of Clapham Hill Dairy – such a shame the large wheel on the handcart disguises the name. The motor van to the right obviously had no trouble in journeying from Clapham Hill, which is situated on the other side of Borstal Hill going towards Canterbury, but what about the chap with the handcart? Or could he have lived locally? Sadly we will never know. Although in the old picture the houses appear to be private residences, today some buildings are replaced and the properties around Goodwin Avenue and out of shot are now businesses.

Heading towards Herne Bay we reach the village of Swalecliffe. This undated postcard incorrectly identified as Swalecliffe Road, Tankerton, is today known as St

Still in Swalecliffe, this 1950s postcard shows the Broadway at Swalecliffe with the Esso garage of Quinney's Auto Services in business from 1952 until 2002. Arthur Quinney originally worked in a Brixton garage in London before moving to Whitstable. No self-service petrol there, only first-class service from staff, even up to closure. Demolition has taken place with the new project rightfully called 'the Quinney', a housing and apartment block still being erected at the time of research. The shopping area comprised then of Greenstead & Sons butchers shop (furthest right), Al Fonsas Vegneris fishmongers at No. 90, The Broadway Stores at No. 88, No. 86 the post office and general stores which in the 1960s was owned by the television and radio entertainer 'cheerful' Charlie Chester. At the end is the Swalecliffe Library as today. Now we have Head over Heals beauty shop,

Pip's fish bar, shop closed and Ron Willis' Swalecliffe post office and stores which was originally in Oxford Street. Motor cars are becoming popular with a Standard 12 identified to the left. In the middle of the picture we see the Wheatsheaf public house from 1932 and rebuilt in 1935. Recent demand meant incorporating a restaurant called 'Hungry Horse' to this very popular establishment.

Before leaving Swalecliffe this undated card is possibly a children's May Day procession that leans towards the post-Edwardian era by the style of dress. The road under the bridge leads to the now Thanet Way. The nearby Swalecliffe and Chestfield railway station opened later in 1928. The old style railway bridge was later replaced with a more solid structure. Interestingly, in recent times despite a clear sign on the bridge today denoting a 13ft 3 in (4m) clearance to road traffic, I remember a double-decker bus getting stuck under it in 2003 with a close inspection today collaborating the event.

Passing under the bridge in the previous picture would lead us to Chestfield. The course stretching over Shrub Hill is home to the Chestfield Golf Club. Mr George Reeves, a builder, purchased 700 acres of land in Chestfield and constructed the golf course. On the site was a fourteenth-century barn, which was originally the club house. The club, reputed to be the oldest in the country, was opened on 5 May 1924 by Abe Mitchell, a professional golfer at the time. These lovely 1920s cars show the elegance surrounding a sport then considered a preserve of the wealthier of the community. Information received reveals that it is an American car to the left and a British Standard car to the right. Petrol during 'the old days' would have been around 1s 4d per gallon. In today's view we have the club house main building and reception, the Barn restaurant and the secretary's office and meeting room.

Shrub Hill Golf Club, Whitstable.

Other local titles published by The History Press

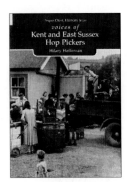

Voices of Kent and Sussex Hop Pickers
HILARY HEFFERNAN

Right up to the late 1950s, the annual hop-picking season provided a welcome escape for thousands of families who lived and worked in the poorer parts of London, who would migrate every year to the hop gardens of Kent and Sussex to pick the harvest. The photographs and reminiscences in this book tell a fascinating story; of hardship, adventures, mishaps, misfortune and laughter experienced during hardworking holidays among the bines.
0 7524 3240 0

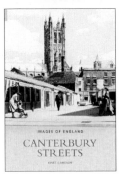

Canterbury Streets
JANET CAMERON

This book examines the streets of Canterbury in an attempt to detail the history of the people and places contained within them and create a sense of the past here. Discover the derivation of the old streets' names, how they have changed and the new routes in this many-layered city. Canterbury Streets will delight those who know the area as it was and those who live in the city today.
0 7524 3398 9

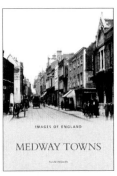

Medway Towns
ALUN PEDLER

Using over 200 images from around the turn of the twentieth century, this book offers a pictorial history of the Medway Towns of Strood, Rochester, Chatham and Gillingham alongside the smaller settlements of Snodland, Halling and Caxton, Cobham and Hingham, the Hoo Peninsula and Rainham and Upchurch. The result is a volume which will delight all those who have fond memories of the area or who wish to know more about the fascinating history of this part of Kent.
0 7524 3303 2

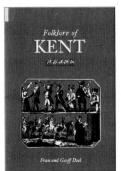

Folklore of Kent
FRAN AND GEOFF DOEL

Kentish folklore reflects the curious geography and administrative history of Kent, with its extensive coastline and strong regional differences between east and west. From saints to smugglers, hop pickers to hoodeners, mummers to May garlands, wife sales to witchcraft, this book charts the traditional culture of Kent as expressed in folklore, legends, customs and songs.
0 7524 2628 1

If you are interested in purchasing other books published by The History Press, or in case you have difficulty finding any of our books in your local bookshop, you can also place orders directly through our website
www.thehistorypress.co.uk